Copyright © 2011 by Ann Peckham.

All rights reserved. No portion of this book, except for brief review, may be reproduced, stored in a retrieval system, or transmitted in any form or by any means- electronic, mechanical, photocopying, recording or otherwise- without written permission of the publisher. For information contact; lulu.com

Cover and some interior photos: Ann Peckham
Some interior photos: Michelle Payne-Gale (MPG), Essence Photography
Cover Photo: Cherry Blossom at the Living Proof Orchard

Disclaimer: The information contained in this booklet is not intended as medical advice. Ann Peckham does not recommend cooked foods or standard medical practices. The author, publisher and/or distributors will not assume responsibility for any adverse consequences resulting from adopting the lifestyle described herein.

Fabulous Cakes, Decadent Desserts and Heart Healthy Chocolates: an exciting adventure into a world of seemingly naughty but exceptionally nice treats that will liven up your diet in the most amazing ways.

Copyright © 2011 by Ann Peckham; Publisher: lulu.com

ISBN- 978-1-4477-8405-0

Table of Contents

Introduction 7
Inside info to help informed choices 8
    Kick the Sugar Blues 8
    Milk not as good for you as you thought * 8
    Coconuts; Better for you than you realise 9
Mooses, Yoghurts and Fruit Salad 11
    Strawberry Yoghurt 11
        Picture 1 Fruit Salad 12
    Black Cherry Moose 13
    Lime Moose 14
Cakes, Pies and Galleta 15
    Carrot Cake 16
    Scrumptious Raw Spicy Apple Pie with Cashew Nut Cream 18
        Picture 2 Apple Pie (photo by MPG) 19
    Cashew cream 19
    Raspberry Sheezecake 20
        Picture 3 Raspberry Sheezecake (photo by MPG) 21
    Strawberry Sheezecake* 22
        Picture 4 Special Birthday Strawberry Sheezecake 23
    Dark Chocolate Galleta 24
        Picture 5 Rich Dark Chocolate Galleta (photo by MPG) 25
    Green Galleta 26
        * Lucuma Powder; 27
        Nutrition 27
        Health Benefits 27
        Picture 6 Green Galleta 27
    Double Chocolate Cherry Sheeze cake* 28
    Perfect Chocolate Moose 30
        Picture 7 Perfect Chocolate Moose 31

Thank you Mum for supporting me, being there and believing that I would become a success.

- Chocolate Orange Sheezecake* 32
    - Picture 8 Chocolate Orange Sheezecake 33
  - White Chocolate Perfections 34
    - Picture 9 White Chocolate Perfection Hearts 35
  - Banoffee Pie 36
    - Picture 10 Banoffee Pie 37
- How to remove the skins from almonds 38
- Chocolates, Fudges and Brownies 39
  - Chocolate Delights 39
    - Picture 11 Chocolate Delight 39
  - Chocolate Coconut Macaroons 40
    - Picture 12 Chocolate Coconut Macaroon 40
  - Chocolate Fudge 41
    - Picture 13 Chocolate Fudge 41
  - Foti Frolics* 42
    - * Mesquite: 42
    - **Fo-Ti: also known as (He Shou Wu) 42
  - Chocolate Brownies 43
  - Coconut Macaroons 44
- These dishes are easier to make than you think 45
  - Student comments (they are mostly "middle aged" women): 45
  - And these are some comments from workshop participants 46
- How to contact Ann 47

Introduction

Living on a restricted diet can be soul destroying when we have had years of denying ourselves some of life's pleasures (cakes, chocolates, biscuits and puddings). This is especially difficult when it feels that this might be forever because every time we give in and indulge we find that we have to pay the price and be even stricter which feels even more depressing.

Don't you hate feeling deprived?

With a strong rebellious streak I really needed to find a way to indulge my decadent side and not have to pay the price.

Now I eat cakes and desserts and chocolates and biscuits every day and haven't put on any weight in 5 years so that must mean that I have found a way to do this in a way that doesn't cause problems.

I love to make fabulous tasting desserts and sharing them with friends but as there is only one of me and many of you I decided that I would share all of my decadent dessert recipes in a book for all of you to be able to make them for yourselves.

We will start off with some really incredibly simple but highly effective puddings that can be made in moments. There is a simple trick that transforms an ordinary fruit salad into an Epicurean Delight. The amazing thing about these is they are so easy to make and taste so fabulous that people find it difficult to accept that they are also beneficial for health, and they are!

Next you will learn how to make some really impressive but again relatively easy cakes and fruit pies. These range from a moist sugar free Carrot Cake right through to a Double Chocolate Cherry Sheezecake and the mind blowing Banoffee Pie.

We will finish off by discovering how easy it is to make healthy chocolates that taste better than shop bought ones and are good for body, heart and mind!

There are several things to keep in mind as you progress through this book and they are outlined on the next page.

Inside info to help informed choices

Kick the Sugar Blues

Why kick sugar? Refined sugar is not a food, regardless of how much more "natural" it is than the packaged chemical substitutes. The process sugar cane is taken through to produce that white stuff Americans are so addicted to is the same process that opium poppies are taken through to produce heroin. This is not a food; it is a drug.

Like all drugs, when you ingest sugar it has profound effects on your body. The moment your body registers that you've eaten sugar, it tells it to fuel itself on the sugar and carbs rather than burn fat for energy.

Sugar picks you up and lets you down ("sugar blues"). It interferes with clear mental processing, natural energy, and normal body rhythms. It is unquestionably linked as a cause of diabetes (along with refined flour). It is addictive! The more you eat, the more you crave. Further, it does nothing to satisfy. Sugary snacks will leave you hungry for more as your body will not recognize that you gave it something to feed itself.

William Dufty's **"Sugar Blues"** ISBN 0-446-34312-9 will give you all of the information you need to convince you that consuming refined sugar is not good for you in any way whatsoever.

Milk not as good for you as you thought *

It's not a good idea to drink milk; most people know it contains fat and cholesterol but did you know it contains the protein CASEIN (which is basically glue which leads to a lot of mucous build-up and other health problems like asthma and congestion).

Milk also contains powerful growth hormones, viruses, a host of chemical and biological bacterial agents, bovine proteins that cause allergies, insecticides, antibiotics and all this contributes to today's problem of obese children and more.

Cow's milk is the number one allergic food in the USA. It has been well documented as a cause in diarrhoea, cramps, irritable bowel syndrome, bloating, gas, gastrointestinal bleeding, iron-deficiency anaemia, skin rashes, atherosclerosis, and acne.

It is the primary cause of recurrent ear infections in children. It has also been linked to insulin dependent diabetes, rheumatoid arthritis, infertility, and leukaemia. Milk and refined sugar make two of the largest contributions to food induced ill health in the US and globally.

*More information in the book "Whitewash, The Disturbing Truth About Cow's Milk and Your Health" by Joseph Keon

Coconuts; Better for you than you realise

Contain no appreciable levels of cholesterol. They increase the speed of the thyroid allowing the body to lose weight and toxins. Coconut oil cannot be stored in the body as fat, it need to be burned on the spot, which fires up our excessive fat burning metabolism.

They support healthy cholesterol formation in the liver as high density lipoprotein (HDL) which is essential to healthy hormone production.

Coconut oil (and all saturated fats) has been blamed for many years as a cause of bad cholesterol levels, which supposedly leads to heart disease. But studies done on traditional tropical populations that consume large amounts of coconut oil show just the opposite. One of the best ways to study the effects of coconut oil on human nutrition is to look at tropical populations that get most of their caloric intake from the saturated fat of coconut oil. Logic would dictate that if the saturated fat/cholesterol theory of heart disease and obesity were correct, those populations with the highest consumption of saturated fats would be the most overweight and have the highest rates of heart disease. Such is not the case.

In a study published in 1981, the populations of two South Pacific islands were examined over a period of time starting in the 1960s, before western foods were prevalent in the diets of either culture. The study was designed to investigate the relative effects of saturated fat and dietary cholesterol in determining serum cholesterol levels. **Coconuts were practically a staple in the diets, with up to 60% of their caloric intake coming from the saturated fat of coconut oil.** The study found very healthy people who were relatively free from the modern diseases of western cultures, including obesity and heart disease. Their conclusion: "Vascular disease is uncommon in both populations and there is no evidence of the high saturated fat intake from coconuts having a harmful effect in these populations."

This situation rapidly altered as the Standard American Diet (SAD) was introduced and the incidence of obesity and heart disease dramatically increased.

All of the decadent delights that are outlined in this book are completely free from refined sugar, they contain no dairy of any sort and for those of you who have intolerance to wheat they are free from that as well. Most of the recipes have coconut oil in them which as you can read above has the beneficial effect of increasing the function of the thyroid which allows the body to rid itself of toxins. So you can feel safe that all of the recipes inside this book will be more beneficial for you to eat than not eat.

Do keep in mind though that if you have succumbed to diabetes then even fruit sugars must be avoided until you have it under control. There is a great book called "There is a Cure for Diabetes" by Gabriel Cousens MD which is a must read for anyone who is suffering with that: ISBN 978-1-55643-691-8

Mooses, Yoghurts and Fruit Salad

Strawberry Yoghurt

I've been told by some of my customers that they have had experience of fruit yoghurts that have been fermented and have been somewhat less than impressed. I've never really got much into the fermenting process which always seems a little hit and miss to me so none of these have to go through that process, which makes them really easy.

Ingredients

- Small punnet of organic strawberries (non-organic ones will have been sprayed with chemicals) Save a few for decoration
- A small handful of cashews (not roasted or salted!)
- ½ cup of organic coconut milk (you can get this in tins)
- Juice of ½ a lemon
- 1Tbs of maple syrup or runny honey or agave nectar (this is extracted from the agave cactus which they use to make Tequila; it has had some controversy in raw circles recently but is better than refined sugar).

Method

- Remove the green end from the strawberries and place them in a blender along with the lemon juice, coconut milk and sweetener and blend till runny.
- Add the cashew nuts and blend till they stop making a clattering noise
- Pour into serving bowls and slice the remaining strawberries and carefully decorate the surface
- Cover and place into a fridge for 30 minutes to firm up a little
- Eat slowly to savour the delight of a real fruit dessert

Fruit Salad

My memories of fruit salads were the sort that came out of a tin and were drenched in syrup or the home-made variety that consisted of banana, orange, grapes and apple. So I avoided them for many years. But now I will have one out of preference virtually every day. I've developed an incredibly simple but enormously effective technique that astounds customers with its effectiveness.

"Cut the fruit up very small"

Ingredients

- Choose from Pineapple; black cherries; nectarines; peaches (peal the skin off, it's too furry!) strawberries; Sharon fruit (experiment, it's fun)
- Small handful of Pecan nuts; cut up finely
- 1Tbs of maple syrup (optional as the fruits create plenty of their own liquid)

Method

- Cut the fruit up into small pieces eg. Cut the strawberries in half then in half again then cut each quarter into three or four pieces. By doing this you ensure that each mouthful has a different combination of fruits and each taste subtly different from the rest
- Mix the fruit together and sprinkle the nuts over it.
- Top off with a cashew nut creem (see Apple Pie for recipe)

Picture 1 Fruit Salad

Black Cherry Moose

Ingredients

- 1 cup of black cherries (you can use frozen ones but please defrost them by standing them in a bowl standing in hot water. This is important otherwise when the melted coconut oil comes into contact with the frozen fruit it will re-solidify)
- 1 handful of cashew nuts
- 2 Tbs honey (or maple syrup or agave nectar), both available in most food shops
- 3 Tbs coconut butter/oil melted
- 2 Tbs coconut milk (you can get this in tins, so choose the organic version)

Method

- Using the blender blend the black cherries with the honey and the coconut milk until it is smooth
- Add the cashew nuts and blend again until smooth
- Add the melted coconut butter and blend till there are no lumps at all
- Pour or spoon into serving bowls and cover with cling film and put into the fridge to set

(You can make a whole range of fruit mooses by changing the fruit, I make strawberry, raspberry, summer fruit, fruits of the forest, black forest fruits (frozen from a supermarket) mango, papaya, pineapple, nectarine or any other favourite soft fruit. This is an area that you can experiment to your heart's content and see what you come up with; let me know if you get a really good one.

Lime Moose

This one is so completely different from the sweeter fruit mooses that it deserves a section all to itself; I learnt how to make this when I trained as a Raw Chef with Peter Pure of www.rawfoodparty.com in 2009. It is a great accompaniment to a "Mexican meal" (this is a more advanced section that will appear in a future book)

Ingredients
- 2 ripe avocadoes
- 2 ripe limes (they are starting to look slightly yellow)
- The zest of the limes
- 2Tbs agave nectar or maple syrup
- ¼ cup of coconut oil (melted by standing it in bowl of hot water)
- 1tsp vanilla extract
- Pinch of Himalayan salt (this is very different to sodium chloride as it has been extracted from the foothills of the Himalayas from seas that existed 250 million years ago, so no pollution and highly mineralised)

Method
- Remove the skin and stone from the avocadoes
- Zest the limes before juicing them, you'll find that rolling them on the work surface for a few moments will make it a little easier to extract the juice. Use one of the hand lemon juicers.
- Add all of the ingredients to a blender and blend till smooth
- Pour into serving dishes and place in the fridge for a couple of hours

Cakes, Pies and Galleta

One of the most upsetting aspects of getting older is the realisation that we can no longer depend on our bodies to deal with the amount of abuse we continuously bombard it with.

We either ignore this at our peril or take measures to counter it.

If we then discover that it is much more difficult to shift that stubborn weight and our energy levels are not as they used to be do we really have to resign ourselves to a life completely bereft of treats?

Thankfully, we do not.

In this section you will find an array of wonderfully decadent cakes and loads of other yummy stuff that you will find it hard to believe are not on the avoid list.

They are much easier to make than the cooked versions and are packed full of nutrients and completely devoid of toxins.

So welcome to the section that will astound and delight you and all of your friends and family.

Carrot Cake

This one is far superior to the sugary wheat based versions you can buy in the supermarket. It is moist and carroty and once you have tasted this you will never want the other version again. It was originally inspired by the excellent book "Eat Smart Eat Raw by Kate (Magic) Wood which is full of great recipes ISBN 1-904010-12-1and was one of the first books on the subject I owned.

Ingredients
- 3 large organic carrots (it is far better to try and always buy or grow organic to reduce your consumption of toxins to the minimum)
- 150g pecans
- 50g fresh or desiccated (unsweetened) coconut
- 2Tbs Date Paste *
- 1 level tsp ginger
- 30g dried apricots soaked for 2 hours (don't buy the orange ones as they have been treated with sulphur to make them stay that colour, choose the brown ones)
- ½ Tbs mixed spice
- ¼ tsp grated nutmeg

Icing
- 60g cashews soaked for 4 hours
- 2 Tbs Honey or Maple syrup
- ½ tsp vanilla extract
- 60 ml filtered water (added slowly as you can't remove it!)

Method
- Juice the carrots; keep the pulp as you are going to use it in the recipe. You can drink the juice as you don't need it in the recipe.
- Drain the apricots and then put them along with the nuts into a food processor and breakdown till it forms a gooey mass.
- Add the date paste* and process again
- Transfer to a large bowl and stir in the carrot pulp and spices till mixed in well.
- Press into a 15cm loose bottomed or spring form cake tin (this will make it so much easier to get out)

Icing

- Drain the cashew nuts and rinse them thoroughly.
- Place them in the blender with the honey/maple syrup and vanilla extract and a little of the water. Blend till smooth adding more water as necessary (you can always add more but you can never take it out!)
- Carefully spread over the top of the carrot cake, cover and place in the fridge for a couple of hours to firm up
- Remove from cake tin and slice up, will serve about 8 people

* Date paste; soak 60 grams of dates in filtered water, just barely covering the dates, over-night. In the morning blend the soaked dates with the soak water and hey presto.

Scrumptious Raw Spicy Apple Pie with Cashew Nut Cream

Ingredients

Base

- 200g Almonds
- 50g each fresh and dried dates
- 25g Coconut butter ; melted

Topping

- 2 Apples peeled, cored and sliced (leave slicing them till last to stop them from going brown)
- 80g Fresh dates
- 1 Dsp mixed spice
- 1 Lemon Juiced Freshly squeezed
- 1 large orange peeled and de-pipped
- ½ inch peeled ginger or ½ tsp dried ginger
- Handful of raisins

Method Base

- Cut the dates up into smaller pieces and place the dried dates with the almonds in the food processor to break them down first
- Then add the fresh dates and coconut oil and process till a dough forms
- Press into a spring form cake tin and refrigerate

Topping
- Put the dates, spice, orange, and lemon juice into to a blender and blend till smooth.
- Then add the raisins and ginger and blend till they are mostly broken down
- Now add the apple slices and blend a little so as not to break them up too much
- Then add some psyillium husks about 2 tsp, this helps to solidify the mixture and stop it sliding off the base.
- Add the topping to the base evenly and smooth with the back of a spoon
- Leave to settle in the fridge for at least 30 minutes

Picture 2 Apple Pie (photo by MPG)

Cashew cream

Ingredients

- 1 cup of cashew nuts soaked for at least 4 hours
- ½ cup of fresh dates (or 2 Tbs maple syrup or runny honey)
- 1 tsp vanilla extract
- Water to desired consistency

Method

- Drain the nuts and blend all the ingredients in the blender (it is important to add the water slowly because it is always possible to add more water but impossible to remove it if it is too runny)
- Serve over or by the apple pie
- If left in the fridge over-night it will thicken slightly and become more like double cream

Raspberry Sheezecake

Base; Ingredients

- 2 cups nuts of choice or mixture (pecans, walnuts, macadamias)
- 1 cup fresh or dried dates pitted and chopped

Method

- Process nuts and dates in the food processor to a sticky consistency.
- Be careful not to over process or you will bring out too much oil.
- Press into a 20cm spring form (or similar) cake tin and put in the fridge to firm up

Filling: Ingredients

- 2 cups raw cashews (soaked for 1 Hour)
- 2 Tbs runny honey,
- ½ cup of melted coconut butter,
- 1 Tbs Lecithin
- 2 tsp vanilla extract.

Method

- Process cashews, honey, and vanilla, in the food processor, to a smooth and creamy consistency, ensure that it really is smooth as this makes all the difference to the finished product, could take up to 5-7 minutes.
- Add the melted coconut oil and process again for 2 minute adding the lecithin about 1 minute into this process
- Pour the filling onto the crust and remove any air bubbles by tapping on the counter.
- Chill until firm, for several hours or over-night.

Topping: Ingredients

- ½ cup Raspberries, frozen,
- tablespoons Agave nectar

Method

- Place raspberries in the food processor with agave nectar and break down to spreadable consistency and spread over the top of the sheeze cake
- Slice the cake and store in the freezer section of the fridge

Defrost for about ½ an hour prior to serving

Picture 3 Raspberry Sheezecake (photo by MPG)

Strawberry Sheezecake*

Base; Ingredients

- 1 cup macadamia nuts
- 1 cup brazils
- 6 Medjool dates

Method

- Process the nuts first till they resemble crumbs then add the dates; removing the stones and chopping them first.
- Do not over process or it will become a paste which you do not want.
- It is good if it still appears to be crumb like as this will give the base a bit of a crunch.
- Press the base evenly into a spring form tin with your fingers, firming it down with the back of a spoon till flat and firm.
- Place in the cool box in the fridge while you make the filling

Filling; Ingredients

- 3 cups cashews soaked in filtered water for a minimum of 3 hours or overnight
- ¼ cup agave nectar (or honey)
- 1 tsp vanilla extract
- 2 Tbs lemon juice freshly squeezed
- 450g strawberries (save some for topping)
- ¼ cup of coconut oil (melted by standing bowl in hot water)
- 4 Tbs Lecithin granules

Method

- Thoroughly drain and rinse the cashews then process them in the food processor till they turn doughy
- Add agave, lemon juice, water and vanilla and process till smooth, this may take some time to ensure that it is.
- Add the lecithin
- Slowly add sliced strawberries then the coconut oil and process till smooth and creamy
- Pour over the base and tap to remove any air bubbles
- Cover and place in freezer for 4 hours

- Remove from freezer add sliced strawberries in an artistic form on the top and then remove from tin and slice, this will make into a minimum of 16 slices
- Place into a sealed container and return to the freezer till needed
- When needed remove from freezer and allow to thaw for 1 hour
- Store in fridge once defrosted otherwise it will become far too soft and sloppy.

Picture 4 Special Birthday Strawberry Sheezecake

*I discovered this recipe on a great website www.PureCalma.com by Renee Lynn Walsh, and adjusted it only very slightly as it is so good

Dark Chocolate Galleta

Base; Ingredients

- 50g Cacao Nibs
- 10g Cacao Powder
- 50g Mesquite*
- 2 Dsp Lucuma* Powder
- 50g Coconut Butter
- 50g Brazil Nuts
- 4 Tbs Agave Nectar (or honey or maple syrup)

Method

- Whilst you are getting on with the rest of the base put the coconut oil/butter to melt by standing a bowl of it in another one containing hot water
- Using a coffee grinder firstly break down the cacao nibs till they make a coarse flour
- Then use the coffee grinder to break down the brazil nuts, you may find cutting them up first will help with this
- In a large mixing bowl add the ground cacao nibs, mesquite, Lucuma, cacao powder and ground brazils and mix well.
- Then add the agave nectar (or honey or maple syrup) and the coconut butter/oil and mix well till everything is combined
- Press down into a spring formed cake base and chill base until solid.

Topping; Ingredients

- 100g Almonds (soaked and skinned see page 38 for the method) or use already blanched almonds, though the taste won't be as good
- 1 ripe Avocado
- 30g raw Cacao Powder
- 2 Tbs Agave Nectar
- 2 Tbs coconut butter melted
- 60 ml Water (you may not need this)

Method

- Put the almonds into the food processor and break down to find bread crumb size
- Put the avocado with the agave nectar (or maple syrup or honey) into a blender and blend till smooth
- Add the almonds and cacao powder and blend again till smooth
- Add the melted coconut butter at this point and blend again
- You will probably find that you don't need to add any water, just see how it goes
- Take the base out of the freezer at this point and allow it to warm at room temperature a little
- When you are happy that the mixture is smooth spread it over the base and smooth over the top, sprinkle with desiccated unsweetened coconut
- Cover and return to the freezer for an hour or so then remove it from the freezer and cut it into serving slices and then return to the freezer. This will ensure that you always have chocolate cake whenever you need it!

Picture 5 Rich Dark Chocolate Galleta (photo by MPG)

I didn't do the decorations they were created by a talented chef called Ricardo, but it looked quite easy to do.

Green Galleta

Ingredients; base

- 50g Raw Coconut Butter (Melted)
- 250g Raw Oat Groats (Milled)
- 2 Dsp Lucuma Powder*
- 75g Raw Cashews (Milled)
- 75g Raisins (Milled Lightly)
- 50g Fresh Coconut Grated

Method

- Mix all the above together and press firmly into Spring Cake Tin.
- Place in the fridge to firm up (this will happen because the coconut butter will solidify when chilled)

Ingredients; topping

- 1 Ripe Mango
- ½ Large Avocado
- 8 Fresh Dates
- 2 Tbs Agave Nectar
- 60 Raw Coconut Butter/oil (melted)
- 100g Almonds (Soaked, Skimmed and Milled)
- 40g Brazil Nuts (Milled)
- 1 tsp Spirulina

Method

- Put the mango and the avocado into the blender first along with the agave nectar and coconut butter blend till liquid then add the rest of the ingredients and continue to blend till all lumps are gone
- Spread over chilled base and smooth out
- Place in Chill Box or Fridge.

* Lucuma Powder;

Lucuma powder is made from the subtropical fruit of the lucuma tree, which is native to Peru, Chile and Equador. The taste is described as maple or caramel to pumpkin-like.

Nutrition

Lucuma provides 14 essential trace elements, including a considerable amount of potassium, sodium, calcium, magnesium and phosphorus,.

Health Benefits

Lucuma has been used for centuries in South America for its medicinal properties. A study concluded that lucuma may have anti-inflammatory, anti-aging and skin-repair effects on human skin.

Picture 6 Green Galleta

Double Chocolate Cherry Sheeze cake*

Base; Ingredients

- 1 ¾ cups almonds
- ½ cup cacao nibs
- Pinch Himalayan salt
- 1 tsp cherry extract
- 1 Tbs cacao powder
- ¾ cup dates

Method

- Grind the cacao nibs in a coffee grinder
- Process the almonds, ground cacao nibs and salt in the food processor until they resemble fine crumbs
- Add the cherry extract and cacao powder and pulse till mixed
- Add the dates and process until the mixture starts to stick together.
- Don't process too long or it will turn into a paste which you do not want to happen
- Press the base evenly into a spring form tin with your fingers, firming it down with the back of a spoon till flat and firm.
- Place in freezer while you make the filling

Filling; Ingredients

- 3 cups cashews soaked for at least 3 hours
- 1 cup of fresh black cherries; stones removed
- 1/3 cup maple syrup
- 6 dates de-stoned
- 2 Tbs fresh lemon juice
- ¼ cup of water (add slowly as may not be needed)
- 2 tsp cherry extract
- ½ cup coconut oil (melted slowly in a bowl standing in hot water)
- ¾ cup cacao powder

Method

- Drain and rinse the and process them with the maple syrup lemon juice and a little water till smooth
- Add the cherries
- Chop the dates add them and process till they are all broken down and mixed in
- You are aiming for a smooth creamy texture so this could take almost 5 minutes to achieve
- Add the cherry extract, coconut oil and cacao powder and process again till smooth
- Pour the filling onto the base and smooth over
- Place back in the fridge to solidify,
- After about 4 hours take out and remove from tin and cut into at least 16 slices
- Place on display plate, cover and replace in fridge or freezer
- If stored in freezer thaw in fridge for at least an hour before serving
- Decorate with fresh black cherry halves before serving

*I adjusted a recipe from www.Bewellbuzz.com to make it easier to understand and moister whilst being less expensive.

Perfect Chocolate Moose

Moose; Ingredients

- 8 dates soaked for 1 hour
- 2Tbs maple syrup
- 2 tsp vanilla extract
- 1 ripe avocado chopped up
- 4 heaped Tbs cacao powder
- 2 Tbs cacao butter melted
- A little filtered water if too stiff

Method

- Place the soaked dates with the sweetener and vanilla into a food processor and process till smooth
- Add the avocado, cacao powder and cacao butter and process till all mixed in
- If it is too stiff add a little water but don't add too much too quickly or it will be too runny

Creem Sauce; Ingredients

- 1 cup cashew soaked for 3 hours (if you get these soaking before you start you won't have to wait for them to be ready!)
- ¼ cup melted coconut oil
- 2 Tbs maple syrup or agave nectar
- 1 tsp vanilla extract

Method

- Drain the cashews and rinse them thoroughly
- Place them into a blender with the rest of the ingredients and blend till smooth

Extra ingredients

- Sliced strawberries or whichever fruit you prefer, maybe a mixture of fresh fruit

Assembly

- Into two tall glasses layer the moose and the sauce adding some of the fruit between each layer, then chill before serving

Picture 7 Perfect Chocolate Moose

Chocolate Orange Sheezecake*

Base; Ingredients

- 1 cup Almonds
- ¼ cup cacao powder
- 1 heaped Dsp Lucuma powder
- 2 Tbs cacao butter melted
- 1 Tbs coconut oil melted
- 6 dates

Method

- Process the nuts first till they resemble crumbs
- Add the cacao powder and the dates making sure that you have removed the stones (this is easy to do if you cut them in half before adding them)
- Do not over process or it will become a paste which you don't want.
- Add the coconut oil and the cacao butter and process till it sticks together
- It's good if it still appears to be crumb like as this will give the base a bit of a crunch.
- Keep back ¼ of the base mixture for the topping
- Press the base evenly into a spring form tin with your fingers, firming it down with the back of a spoon till flat and firm.
- Place in fridge while you make the topping

Topping; Ingredients

- 2 ½ cups cashews soaked in filtered water for a minimum of 3 hours or overnight
- ¼ cup agave
- ¼ cup maple syrup
- 2 Oranges
- ¾ cup of coconut oil (melted by standing bowl in hot water)
- ½ tsp orange essential oil

Method

- Grate the zest off the oranges
- Squeeze the juice out of the zested oranges

- Place the cashews (drained and rinsed), agave, coconut butter, zest, essential oil and orange juice in the food processor and process until very smooth
- Pour over the base and tap to remove any air bubbles
- Place in the cool box in the fridge to firm up for 1 hour
- Then evenly sprinkle the set aside base mixture over the top
- Cover and place in freezer for 4 hours
- Remove from freezer and remove from tin and slice into a minimum of 16 slices
- Place on serving plate, cover and return to the freezer till needed
- When needed remove from freezer and allow to thaw for 1 hour
- Store in fridge

Picture 8   Chocolate Orange Sheezecake

* This recipe was originally inspired by Susan Powers on the website www.Rawmazing.com

White Chocolate Perfections

Base; Ingredients

- ¼ cup coconut butter, melted in the usual way
- 2 Tbs cacao powder
- 2 Tbs Agave nectar or maple syrup
- ½ cup coconut flakes
- ¼ cup cacao nibs (available on line or in very good health food stores)
- ½ tsp vanilla extract
- Pinch of Himalayan salt

Method

- Grind the cacao nibs in a coffee grinder until they are almost powder, with still some little bits visible
- Grind the coconut flakes until they are little bits
- Add all of the base ingredients to the melted coconut butter and mix well
- Press firmly into a spring form cake tin and put into fridge to firm up

White Chocolate topping; Ingredients

- ½ cup cashews soaked for 2 hours
- 2 Tbs agave nectar or maple syrup
- 2Tbs Cacao Butter melted (this works best if you grate the cacao butter; this can be done with a sharp knife; then place in a bowl that is standing in hot water)
- 1 tsp vanilla extract
- 1 tsp coconut oil, melted
- ¼ tsp fresh lemon juice

Method

- Place the liquids into the blended first then the cashews on top of that and blend till smooth.
- You may find you need to add a little filtered water to help it turn over but don't add it unless it is necessary
- Pour over the base and place in fridge to solidify

Topping; Ingredients
- ½ cup fresh raspberries
- 1 tsp maple syrup

Method

- Place in a bowl and mash with the back of a fork
- Apply to the surface of the white chocolate, cover and return to the fridge for storage.

Picture 9 White Chocolate Perfection Hearts

Banoffee Pie

(This recipe has been lusted after and now you can have it!)

Base; Ingredients

- 1 cup almonds
- 1 ½ cups dates

Method

- Place the almonds into the processor and break down until the oil starts to exude, this may take some time
- Cut the dates into quarters and add to the almonds and continue to process until it starts to stick together
- Press firmly into a spring form base and place in fridge while you make the rest

Filling; Ingredients

- 1 cup cashews soaked for 4 hours
- 3 ripe bananas
- 2 Tbs coconut oil melted
- ¼ cup filtered water if necessary

Method

- Place the peeled and chopped bananas into a blender
- Drain and rinse the cashews and add on top of the bananas and the coconut oil
- Blend until smooth

Caramel Sauce; Ingredients

- ¼ cup Coconut sugar
- ½ cup un-soaked cashews
- 2 Tbs maple syrup
- 1 tsp vanilla extract

Method

- Blend until smooth and sticky

Topping of chopped pecan nuts mixed with a little maple syrup

Assembly

- Remove the base from the fridge and spread the caramel sauce evenly over the surface
- Pour the banana mix on to this whilst it is still within the spring form base, this will ensure that it retains its form
- Return to the fridge for an hour or so then sprinkle the topping over the top for a crunchy delightful finish

Picture 10 Banoffee Pie

How to remove the skins from almonds

- Soak almonds in filtered water over night
- Once the almonds have been soaked over-night drain them off and add hot water for 2-3 minutes.
- Carefully drain off the water, so you don't burn yourself, and add cold water.
- Test to see if the skins will come off easily, by squeezing one
- If not then pour off the cold water and add hot water for another 2 minutes or so
- Pour off the water and add cold again. (this has the effect of stretching and shrinking the skins so that they will be easy to get off)
- Remember to squeeze the almonds pointed end in towards your hand because if you don't you'll be chasing them all around the kitchen

Chocolates, Fudges and Brownies

These will require some less usual ingredients all of which are accessible from on line stores; I've even found them on eBay and Amazon. You will find that there are heated discussions on line about whether some things are truly raw or not. As long as it hasn't been loaded down with sugar and exposed to high levels of heat and had chemicals added to it then it is better than the main stream products available in most shops. So if you are making them for yourself with ingredients you have carefully selected you know that they will be better for you than the usual suspects.

Chocolate Delights

Ingredients

- 1 cup cacao powder
- ½ cup maple syrup
- ½ cup coconut butter melted

Method

- Place the maple syrup and the melted coconut butter into a blender then add the cacao powder and blend till thoroughly mixed.
- Pour into a shallow dish and put into the fridge for about 5 hours
- Take out of the fridge and using a teaspoon scoop out truffle sized bits and roll them into balls.
- Dip them in cacao powder or desiccated (unsweetened) coconut and return them to the fridge for keeping

Picture 11 Chocolate Delight

Chocolate Coconut Macaroons

Ingredients; makes 20 or more

- 2 cups Coconut flakes
- 1 cup cacao powder
- ½ cup honey or maple syrup
- ¼ cup coconut butter melted
- 1 tsp vanilla extract
- Pinch Himalayan salt

Method

- In a food processor place all of the dry ingredients and pulse to mix them together. You don't want to break the coconut flakes down too much.
- Tip into a mixing bowl and add the liquid ingredients mixing them in thoroughly
- Using a teaspoon scoop out enough to make little clusters, you **don't** want to form them into balls.
- Place on a tray and put them in the fridge for an hour or so before serving

Picture 12 Chocolate Coconut Macaroon

Chocolate Fudge

Ingredients

- ½ cup cashews soaked for 1 hour
- ½ cup cacao powder
- 2 Tbs coconut butter melted
- 2 Tbs cacao butter melted
- 2 Tbs Mesquite *Try maca instead? Try carob?*
- 6 dates cut into quarters
- 1 tsp vanilla extract
- Pinch Himalayan salt

Method

- Drain and rinse the cashews and place all the ingredients into a blender
- Blend till smooth, you may have to add a little water to help it turn over but only a little at a time
- Roll into balls and cover with whatever takes your imagination
- Store in the fridge and nibble as you get the desire

Picture 13 Chocolate Fudge

Foti Frolics*

Ingredients

- 1 cup cacao powder
- ¼ cup Mesquite*
- ¼ cup Maca
- ½ cup Almond butter
- ¾ cup mixed maple syrup and honey
- 2 Tbs Fo-ti**
- 2 heaped Tbs Lucuma powder
- 1 Tbs vanilla extract
- Pinch Himalayan salt

Method

- Process everything except the Lucuma powder in the food processor until well blended and very stiff
- Place into a large bowl and knead in the Lucuma powder until it is no longer sticky
- Roll into logs or little balls and wrap in gold foil and store in the cool box of the fridge

* **Mesquite:**

Is an excellent source of protein along with containing high quantities of calcium, magnesium, potassium, iron and zinc; it is also rich in the amino acid lysine. In addition to its great taste, the major benefits of Mesquite Powder include high dietary fibre content .The result is a food with the ability to stabilize your blood sugar levels. Mesquite keeps hunger at bay!

**Fo-Ti: also known as (He Shou Wu)

Its root is a common herb supplement in China. Traditional Chinese Medicine believes Fo-Ti can help them with greying hair, anti-aging, vaginal discharge, and erectile problems. They also think it can boost their energy, enhance their liver, kidney etc. Researches revealed Fo-Ti could lower serum cholesterol, decrease hardening of the arteries, and improve immune function.

*I found this recipe on the website www.rawfoodtalk.com one Halloween and it was a huge success

Chocolate Brownies

Ingredients

- 1 cup walnuts
- ¾ cup almonds
- 12 moist dates
- 1/3 cup cacao powder
- 1/3 cup cacao nibs
- ½ tsps. vanilla extract
- 2 tsps. maple syrup
- Pinch of Himalayan salt

Method

- Set aside ¼ cup of walnuts and chop them up
- Place the rest of the nuts into a food processor and process till resemble bread crumbs
- Grind the cacao nibs in a coffee grinder and add to the nuts
- Add the cacao powder and vanilla extract to the nuts and process again
- Chop the dates in half and add them one at a time through the shoot of the food processor till the mixture starts to clump together
- Then add the maple syrup and process briefly
- Turn out into a large mixing bowl and stir in the remaining walnuts by hand. You may need to work quite hard to achieve this but it is great exercise!
- Press the mixture into a square dish making sure that you press it in firmly, I find that using the back of a dessert spoon works well
- Place into the fridge to chill and cut into squares to serve.

These are delicious and if you keep them in the fridge they should last at least 10 days if they last that long and they are so good for you.

Coconut Macaroons

This one uses a dehydrator but as some of my clients really want this recipe I cannot deny them it in a book of this title!

Ingredients

- 2 cups fresh coconut
- 10 dates
- 2 cups of filtered water
- 1 tsp vanilla essence

Method

- If you have a masticating juicer pass the coconut through it with the blanking plate on. If not then you can do everything in the food processor
- Place all ingredients in food processor. You don't want to over process this as you will want the coconut to still be recognisable
- Spoon onto Excalibur's teflex sheets as round cookies
- Flatten to ¼ inch thickness,
- Dehydrate at 100F for 24-36 hours.
- Turn over and remove the teflex sheet about half way through
- Check them at 24 hours to see how they are doing and choose when to stop the process when they are at the crunchiness you desire
- The dryer they are the longer they will keep but I doubt whether they will last that long anyway!

These dishes are easier to make than you think

When you share these creations with your friends and families they will be amazed at how fabulous they all taste and even more amazed that they can eat them without the same problems caused by eating the full fat, wheat based sugary versions.

You may think that some of them are too difficult for you to attempt but as my students will tell you they have been astounded by how easy they are to make.

Student comments **(they are mostly "middle aged" women):**

"Here are a few words that show how I have found my experience of your non-cookery course.

I love food, all sorts of food. There has always been room for improvement to my diet. Previously a few days could go by without me eating vegetables, so I knew that something had to change…..

The classes are relaxed and friendly, and Ann gives clear and easy to remember instructions. On top of that **the raw food was far tastier and easier to prepare than I could ever have imagined; and I find it easy to prepare the foods at home.** *I enjoy raw meals and green smoothies almost every day. The potential for a healthier life is just a meal or two away.*
The more I have learnt about eating a healthy raw diet, the more I want to find out.
My new raw additions to my life are so tasty I don't want to turn back. I just want to have more of these delicious recipes.
And all I wanted was to find a better way to add healthy vegetables to my life." Kathy H

"……You are very knowledgeable, passionate and able to communicate the raw food message very effectively but not in a way that alienates people.
Your recipes taste fantastic and are VERY easy to make. It is obvious that you live what you teach. *I*

liked the fact that most of the recipes called for everyday "normal" ingredients….."

Caroline

And these are some comments from workshop participants

*Today's workshop has been inspiring. Filled with **amazing energising food**-wise information- love and laughter.
You sparkle Ann! " T.S.*

*"Fantastic! really enjoyable and inspiring and thought provoking. **Came away knowing that I could start implementing raw foods into my life. Oh yes! the food was fabulous"** W.T.*

*"An interesting and rewarding day. The time passed very quickly. **The food was delicious** and the activities were inspiring and thought provoking" V. M.*

*"Ann's workshop is professional and inspiring. Ann has shown that **raw food recipes are easy to make** and I am looking forward to integrating them into my diet" R.H.*

" I found the assortment of raw food in the most enjoyable. It is amazing what can be achieved without resorting to the use of meat and poultry" H.M.

How to contact Ann

There are many different opportunities to experience the delights of the uncooked world and if you would like to keep informed of the events, activities, launches and offers then please register your interest on the website.

www.sparklingenergy.co.uk

This won't inundate you with newsletters; I'm not that prolific. What it will do though is ensure that you are the first to know of anything new I think would interest you.

I would love to hear of any successes you have with the creation of the recipes in this book. To hear of how your friends and family have been delighted with what you have presented them with and how that made you feel.

Please email me with any stories to

purpleann57@yahoo.co.uk

The next book will be "Recipes to Impress your Non-Raw Guests" or a similar title

Love and light

Ann

Printed in Great Britain
by Amazon.co.uk, Ltd.,
Marston Gate.